River
Food Chains

Angela Royston

Raintree is an imprint of Capstone Global Library Limited, a company incorporated in England and Wales having its registered office at 7 Pilgrim Street, London, EC4V 6LB – Registered company number: 6695582

www.raintreepublishers.co.uk
myorders@raintreepublishers.co.uk

Edited by Claire Throp, Diyan Leake and Helen Cox Cannons
Designed by Joanna Malivoire and Philippa Jenkins
Original illustrations © Capstone Global Library Ltd 2014
Picture research by Elizabeth Alexander and Tracy Cummins
Production by Victoria Fitzgerald
Originated by Capstone Global Library Ltd
Printed and bound in China

ISBN 9781 4062 8419 5
18 17 16 15 14
10 9 8 7 6 5 4 3 2 1

British Library Cataloguing in Publication Data
A full catalogue record for this book is available from the British Library.

Acknowledgements
We would like to thank the following for permission to reproduce photographs: Alamy pp. 12 (© Datacraft – Sozaijiten), 13, 23e, 25 algae (© Trevor Pearson), 16 (© John Warburton-Lee Photography), 20 (© Juniors Bildarchiv GmbH), 23b (© Neil McNicoll), 23d (© WildPictures), 25 salmon (© Alaska Stock), 27 (© Wildscape), 29 (© blickwinkel); Corbis pp. 21 (© Wim van Egmond/Visuals Unlimited), 25 otter (© Joe McDonald), 25 trout (© Ken Lucas/ Visuals Unlimited Inc), 28 (© Philippe Henry/First Light); Getty Images pp. 19 (DeAgostini), 22 (Flickr RF), 25 crayfish (Steve Maslowski); Shutterstock pp. 1 (© Igor Kolos), 4 (© zebra0209), 5 (© Greg Amptman), 7 (© bumihills), 8 (© karamysh), 9 (© Nancy Bauer), 10 (© Christopher Elwell), 11a (© Jan Gottwald), 11b (© Pinosub), 11c (© knin), 11d, 24, 25 fly larva, 25 snail (© scubaluna), 14 (© anotherlook), 15 (© EBFoto), 17a (© Patrick K. Campbell), 17b (© defpicture), 17c (© Santi Rodriguez), 18 (© Johan Swanepoel/Sergey Uryadnikov), 23a (© S Kolesnikov), 23c (© EcoPrint), 25 eagle (© Serjio74), 26 (© Erni); SuperStock p. 17d (© Stock Connection).

Cover photograph of an eagle fish reproduced with permission of Shutterstock (wildpix).

We would like to thank Michael Bright for his invaluable help in the preparation of this book.

Contents

Some words are shown in bold, **like this.**
You can find out what they mean by
looking in the glossary.

Living in a river

Rivers begin in hills or mountains. Streams pour downhill and join together to make a river. The river flows more slowly as it crosses flatter land until it reaches the sea, or a lake.

A river begins as a mountain stream.

A manatee lives in slow-moving rivers.

Many animals and plants live and grow in rivers. This book looks at how they need each other to survive.

World's biggest rivers

This map shows the world's longest rivers. Some rivers, such as the Amazon River in South America, have other rivers that flow into them. As well as these mighty rivers, there are thousands of smaller rivers.

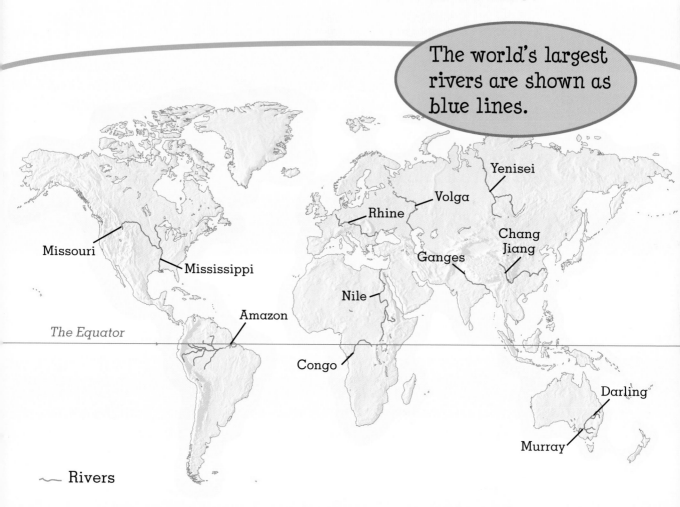

The world's largest rivers are shown as blue lines.

Missouri

Mississippi

Rhine

Volga

Yenisei

Chang Jiang

Ganges

Nile

Amazon

The Equator

Congo

Darling

Murray

〜 Rivers

Longest river

The River Nile flows 6,650 kilometres (4,132 miles) from central Africa across the Sahara Desert to the Mediterranean Sea.

What is a food chain?

All living things need food because it gives them **energy**. Without energy they could not breathe, **digest** food or swim.

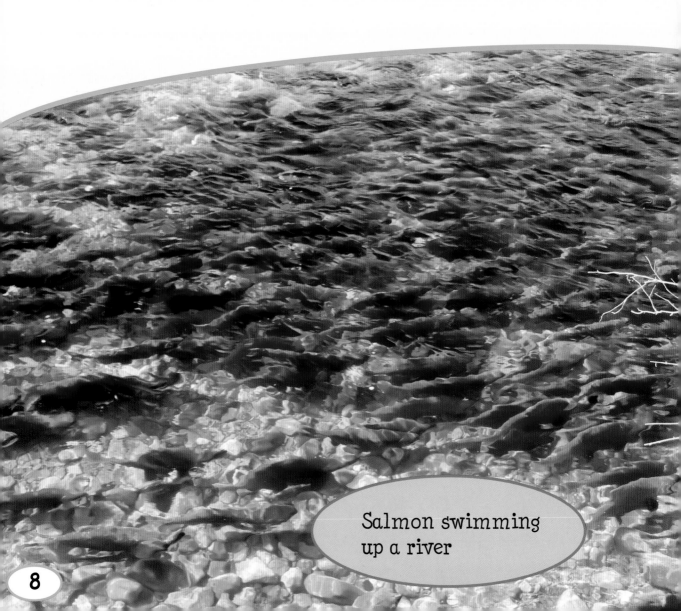

Salmon swimming up a river

Ducks use their bills to get food from the water.

A river **food chain** shows what eats what in the river. The energy in food is passed from plants to each of the animals in the chain.

A European food chain

Many different types of living things form a **food chain**. Otters, trout, caddis flies and pondweed in rivers in Great Britain and Europe form this food chain. **Energy** from the plants passes to the young caddis fly and on to the trout and otter. Without the plants the whole chain would collapse.

The River Severn flows through part of Great Britain.

Food chain

An otter grabs a trout

A trout snatches a young caddis fly

A young caddis fly feeds on river plants

Pondweed grows in rivers

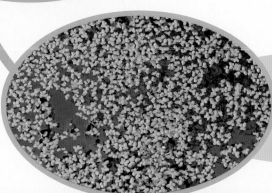

Where do food chains begin?

The European river **food chain** begins with plants because plants make their own food. They use sunlight to make sugar, which feeds the whole plant.

Many plants grow in slow moving rivers.

Too much algae can choke a river with green slime.

Rivers everywhere also contain plants, **algae** and **plankton**. Plants, algae and plankton are called **producers** because they make their own food.

Animal consumers

Animals cannot make their own food. They are called **consumers** because they have to find food in their **habitat** to eat.

A muskrat is an omnivore but it mostly eats plants.

A heron catches a fish to eat.

Herbivores are animals such as caddis flies and manatees that eat mostly plants. **Carnivores**, such as otters and herons, hunt fish or other animals. Some animals, such as muskrats, eat both plants and animals. They are called **omnivores**.

An Amazon food chain

Anacondas, caiman and piranhas all live in the River Amazon. Piranhas are **omnivores** because they eat seeds and flesh. This **food chain** shows how **energy** passes from the seeds to the piranha, then to the caiman and anaconda.

The Amazon River

Food chain

A huge anaconda can swallow a caiman

A caiman swallows a piranha

Piranhas feed on seeds that have fallen into the water

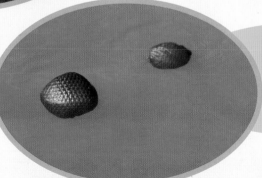

Seeds float on the river

Top predators

An anaconda is too big and strong to be hunted by other animals in the Amazon. It is called a top **predator** because it is at the top of its **food chain**. Crocodiles and snapping turtles are top predators in other rivers.

These two crocodiles are on the River Nile.

This snapping turtle eats all kinds of prey, even baby alligators.

Top predators are fierce, but there are always fewer of them than their **prey.** If predators ate up all their prey, they would have nothing left to eat and would soon starve!

Living on the remains

Piranha fish, snapping turtles and crayfish are **scavengers** as well as **predators**. Scavengers eat the flesh of dead animals.

Crayfish live in the River Danube in Europe.

Flatworms are decomposers.

Snails, freshwater crabs and flatworms are called **decomposers**. They feed on the remains of dead plants and break them up into tiny bits. Before long, every part of the dead plants and animals is cleared away and recycled.

A Limpopo food chain

The Limpopo River flows across southern Africa. In this **food chain**, **energy** passes from **algae** through the caddis fly to the bullfrog, the yellowfish and up to the fish eagle. Animals in a food chain are more likely to be eaten when they are young and not fully formed.

The Limpopo River

Food chain

A fish eagle grabs a small yellowfish

A yellowfish snatches a young African bullfrog

A bullfrog feeds on caddis flies

Young caddis flies feed on algae

Algae makes its own food in the river

23

Food webs

A **food chain** shows one way in which various plants and animals in a **habitat** are linked. However, most animals eat more than one type of food. A **food web** shows how several animals in a habitat are connected. Opposite is a food web in North America.

Freshwater snails feed on **algae**. The food web opposite shows what feeds on the snails.

Food web

American river otter

bald eagle

trout

salmon

freshwater snail

American crayfish

caddis fly larva

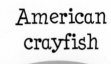

algae

Broken chains

When American crayfish were brought into some British rivers they almost wiped out the local crayfish. This was because American crayfish carry a disease that kills British crayfish.

An American crayfish crawls out of a British river.

A European crayfish

American crayfish are bigger and fiercer than their European cousins. They damage **food chains** by gobbling up so many water plants, small fish and snails that there is little food left for other animals.

Protecting food chains

People damage **food chains**. Chemicals
from farmland and factories pollute
the water. Cutting down trees on the
riverbanks destroys the **habitat** for
beavers and other river animals.

Few animals live in
polluted rivers.

A beaver chews up twigs to make a dam.

People try to protect rivers. For example, beavers have been brought back to some rivers. The beavers' dams create pools, where plants and small animals become food for otters, heron and fish.

Glossary

algae tiny living things in, for example, green slime. Algae can make their own food.

carnivore animal that eats only the meat of other animals

consumer living thing, particularly an animal, that feeds on other living things, such as plants and other animals

decomposer living thing, such as an earthworm, fungus or bacterium, that breaks up the remains of plants and animals and turns them into soil

digest break up food into tiny pieces inside the body

energy power needed to do something, such as move, breathe or swallow

food chain diagram that shows how energy passes from plants to different animals

food web diagram that shows how different plants and animals in a habitat are linked by what they eat

habitat place where something lives

herbivore animal that eats only plants

omnivore animal that eats plants and animals

plankton tiny plants and animals that float near the surface of water

predator animal that hunts other animals for food

prey animal hunted for food

producer living thing, such as a plant, that makes its own food

scavenger animal that feeds off the flesh and remains of dead animals

Find out more

Books
Food Chains (Cycles in Nature), Theresa Greenaway (Wayland, 2014)

River (Life Cycles), Sean Callery (Kingfisher, 2012)

River Food Chains (Protecting Food Chains), Rachel Lynette (Raintree, 2011)

River Story (Read and Discover), Meredith Hooper (Walker Books, 2010)

Websites
www2.sese.uwa.edu.au/swan4kids/mpfoodchain.html
This website looks at food chains and food webs based on the Swan River in Australia.

www.cornwallriversproject.org.uk/education/ed_cd/background/diversity/bo6d.htm
A website that gives examples of food chains and information to help you work out your own food chains.

www.sciencekids.co.nz/sciencefacts/earth/rivers.html
This website designed for children gives lots of fun facts about rivers, with links to the Amazon and other rivers.

www.ypte.org.uk/environmental/rivers/96
Find out all about rivers from beginning to end on this website of the Young People's Trust for the Environment.

Index